Safe with God

BIBLE CHAPTERS FOR KIDS

When I stay close to the Lord, I can rest and be at peace.

"He that dwells in the secret place of the most High will abide under the shadow of the Almighty."

(verse 1)

I know that I can trust the Lord, because He protects me and makes me strong.

"I will say of the Lord, He is my refuge and my fortress: my God; in Him will I trust."
(verse 2)

The Lord can protect me from those who want to hurt me, and can keep me healthy.

"Surely He will deliver you from the snare of the fowler, and from the deadly pestilence."
(verse 3)

The Lord covers me, like a bird covers its baby. He guards me faithfully.

"He will cover you with his feathers, and under his wings will you trust: His truth will be your shield and buckler."

(verse 4)

I don't have to be afraid of the dark, nor of anything during the day.

"You will not be afraid for the terror by night; nor for the arrow that flies by day;"
(verse 5)

I don't have to fear sickness, because the Lord is with me.

"Nor for the pestilence that walks in darkness; nor for the destruction that strikes at midday."

(verse 6)

Even if there is war or chaos all around me, I can feel safe with the Lord.

"A thousand will fall at your side, and ten thousand at your right hand; but it will not come near you."

(verse 7)

I see what happens to those who do wrong things, so I don't want to copy them.

"Only with your eyes will you behold and see the reward of the wicked."
(verse 8)

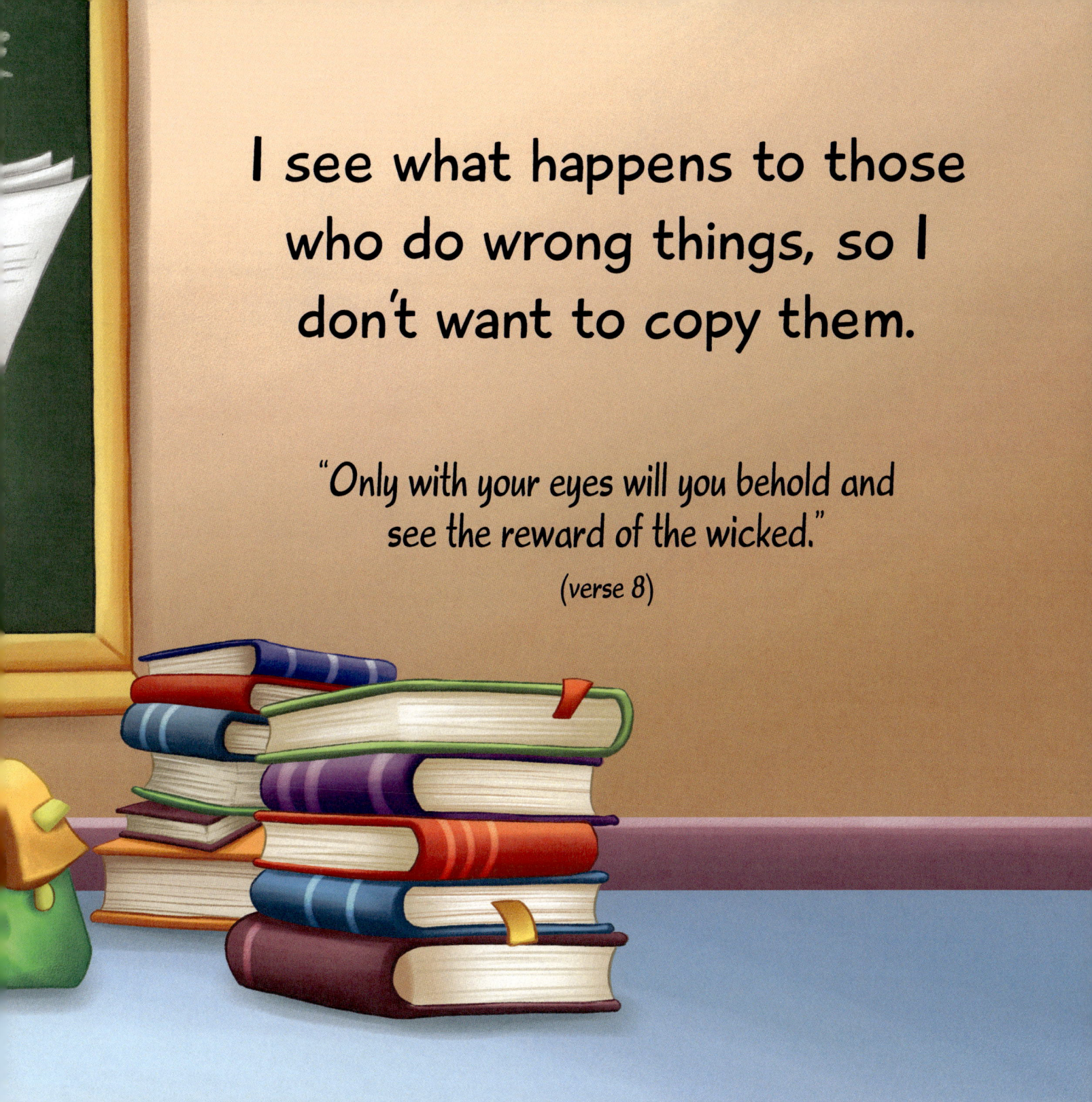

The Lord protects me like a fortress, so when I am with Him, nothing can harm me.

"Because you have made the Lord, which is my refuge, even the most High, your habitation; There will no evil befall you, now will any plague come near your dwelling."

(verse 9,10)

The Lord tells His angels to be my body guards wherever I go.

"For He will give His angels charge over you, to keep you in all your ways."
(verse 11)

They watch over me, so I don't get hurt.

"They will hold you up in their hands, lest you dash your foot against a stone."
(verse 12)

The Lord's angels are strong enough to help me even in dangerous places.

"You will tread on the lion and adder: the young lion and the dragon will you trample under feet." (verse 13)

The Lord loves me, and I love Him. That's why He wants to keep me safe.

"Because he has set his love on Me, therefore will I deliver him: I will set him on high, because he has known My name."

(verse 14)

The Lord says that when I pray and call out to Him, that He will come and rescue me.

"He will call on Me, and I will answer him: I will be with him in trouble; I will deliver him, and honour him." (verse 15)

The Lord loves to care for me so that I can live a long and healthy life with Him.

"With long life will I satisfy him, and show him My salvation."
(verse 16)

More books in the series:

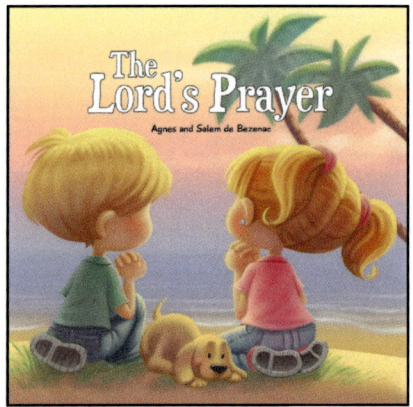 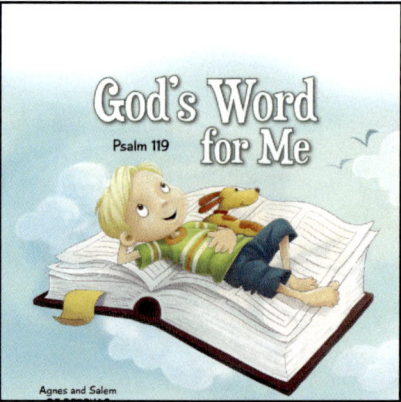 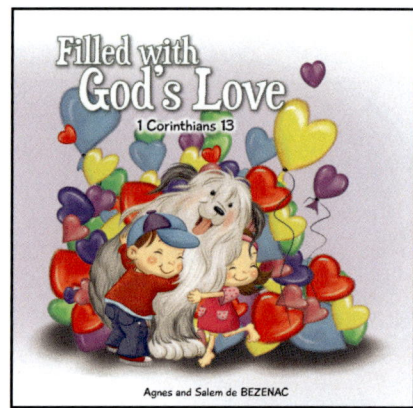

iCHARACTER

Published by iCharacter Ltd. (Ireland)
www.icharacter.org
By Agnes and Salem de Bezenac
Illustrated by Agnes de Bezenac
Colored by Henny Y.
Copyright. All rights reserved.
All Bible verses adapted from the KJV.

Copyright © 2012 by iCharacter Limited. All rights reserved. No part of this book may be reproduced in any form or by any electronic or mechanical means, including information storage and retrieval systems, without written permission from the publisher or author, except in the case of a reviewer, who may quote brief passages embodied in critical articles or in a review.

Made in the USA
Middletown, DE
09 January 2022